The Project:
A story of addictions overcome by faith

By
LB FRENCH

StoryTerrace

Text Duane Noriyuki, on behalf of Story Terrace

Design Grade Design and Adeline Media

Copyright © LB French Second print September 2019

StoryTerrace

www.StoryTerrace.com

Table of Contents

1

THE GRATEFUL DEAD

My life can best be described in sounds. Laughter, cries, prayers, the sound of a referee's whistle, the rush of a snowboard's edge in deep Colorado powder. So, what better place to begin my story than with the sounds of the timeless, inspirational rock'n'roll of The Grateful Dead.

On July 14, 2018, my wife and I were on our way from our home in Frisco, Colorado, to Boulder to see the Grateful Dead & Co., an offshoot of the original band. In my mind they were never the same after Jerry Garcia died in 1995, but he left behind a legacy, an entire culture, based upon his music and persona.

I have seen the Dead more than 125 times during the past 25 years. My first show was in 1979 in Baltimore. Over the years, memories of those concerts have melded into a haze; but on that day, basking in the comradery of over 14,000 kindred Dead Heads, I saw with virgin eyes and listened with virgin ears. For the first time, I was seeing them without being stoned.

I am 58 years old. I smoked marijuana every day for 42 years. Up until a year ago, it was my life's remote control. I could switch it on and off, pause, change channels, mute. Marijuana was a part of everything I did. It was my best friend, and it went everywhere I went. It was part of everything I did, and it controlled when I did it. It was who I was and a staple in my life that ended up nearly destroying my marriage of 26 years.

The concert was part of my awakening, my sobriety. It tested my resolve because I figured that if I could go to a Dead concert without being stoned, I was probably going to be OK. We had been to Folsom Field to see the Dead a few times, and we always sat in the same area on the east side, facing west. As we took our seats, I was amazed as I looked down at the stadium and saw the huge cloud of smoke rising to the sky. Everybody was smoking.

It's hard to see a cloud if you're in one, so I never stopped to wonder how much marijuana was a part of a Dead concert. I thought it was part of the creed, and that getting high was a required Grateful Dead state of impairment, but it turned out that wasn't the case at all. Because tonight straight, I felt more alive, more in tune than ever during that concert. I didn't know how life could have been more beautiful. But then I witnessed the sun setting over the Rocky Mountains, and I swore I could hear Jerry.

We attended the concert with some friends who were in their mid-twenties. One of them was the oldest son of a rugby buddy from back east. Rugby changed my life in the way that unexpected moments like tonight. Come along at the exact point in time you need them. The first time I stepped onto the pitch I felt the sport's flow, its demand for intelligence, fitness, and teamwork. It was like finding a home. I played for over twenty years then coached for another fifteen-plus years.

Rugby love transcends generations. In my life, the sport became a conduit for friendship, careers, and even love. I belonged on the pitch as much as I belonged in Folsom Field that night, singing, dancing, and celebrating a new life.

During the concert, one of our young friends said, "You two are the coolest couple my girlfriend and I have ever seen. We hope that our future can be as happy and fun and successful and cool as yours."

My wife and I looked at each other choking back laughter. He knew nothing about what we had just gone through over the last year, how terribly bad our lives were just a short period of time before, and how we worked fiercely to save our marriage.

It's a wonderful sound—laughter. When the laughter dies, as it did with us, it leaves behind a void that often cannot be occupied by anything other than heartbreak, doubt, and regret; but when laughter returns, it rings truer than before, more authentic, and spontaneous.

Maybe that's what it came down to when we lay with eyes closed and no air left in our lungs. We stopped laughing. We could have walked away from each other, which is what most couples would have done. We could have left the void unfilled, but we chose not to. And our reward was a sunset in Boulder, leading to the excitement of darkness, a different kind of darkness, one that doesn't settle beneath the skin.

"Someday life will be sweet like a rhapsody

When I paint my masterpiece."

It's a Bob Dylan song covered by the Dead. The lyrics meant more that night than ever before. My masterpiece is a love story reflecting barriers faced and my pot addiction I was able to overcome. What saved our marriage was a four-day retreat in Sedona, where our lives, individually and as a couple, were examined from the perspective of a shaman, psychic, marriage counselors, psychiatrists, healers, a guide referred to as our angel, and God.

"Three things cannot be long hidden: the sun, the moon, and the truth." That could be Jerry talking, but it's not. It's a Buddhist quote that has given us insight and direction. It's helped us recognize the importance of giving and nurturing truth in a relationship, no matter how painful it might be. Truth is a gift that we all deserve.

If truth and love made sounds, they would come from my wife's guitar and the songs she writes and sings. They tell stories from her heart, which I have broken numerous times in various ways. I try to trust that I will never do it to her again.

There's one more sound that explains how, after so much turmoil, we were able to forgive each other and move forward as a team. You might think I'm crazy.

But one day while I was walking my dog Kimba, the voices returned.

Grateful Dead, Stanley Mouse Copyright 1989

2

ROCKY MOUNTAIN HIGH AND LOW

Frisco, Colorado, is a mountain town of fewer than 3,000 residents in the heart of Colorado Ski Country.

It is within a short drive to Breckenridge, Keystone, Vail, Copper Mountain, Arapahoe Basin, and other skiing and wildlife areas. When not clogged with traffic, Denver is a little more than an hour to the east.

The town exists because of tourism. People are drawn to its natural beauty and outdoor offerings. Before moving here, my primary relationship with snow involved a shovel, not a snowboard. Our mountains were skyscrapers, and our creeks were gutters.

My wife lived in Breckenridge with a friend for a year after graduating from college. She also visited Colorado when she was growing up. For as long as I have known her, she has yearned to live in Colorado. One year before we made the move here, she took me to Aspen, and after a few days, I, too, fell in love with it. I work virtually, so when my employer told me I could live wherever I wanted as long as it was west of the Mississippi, there was no question where we would end up.

Frisco, however, is a departure from my early life in Ohio, Pennsylvania, and Maryland. The people who come here are people who can afford to come here. They fly into Denver, rent Audis, and buy their kids every T-shirt they see. That would not have been my family. We couldn't afford vacations because we couldn't even afford a new car. We weren't meant to see places like Frisco.

I remember when I was in sixth grade. It was a Saturday afternoon, and my mom and dad took me with them to the car dealership, because Dad needed to buy a new car. We checked out a few cars, test drove a couple of them until he settled on one. We went into the sales office, and I remember the salesman looking at my father and saying, "I'm sorry, but you can't afford the car. Your credit is not good enough."

There was a look of embarrassment on my father's face, and he told the salesman to check again. The salesman showed him some papers. I had never before seen that look on my father's face. He didn't say a word until later that afternoon, when I heard my mother's screams.

I work as an education consultant at a software company. In many ways it's an ideal job. I work from home, so every time I step out of my office in the spare bedroom, I look out the window and see wildlife, mountains, and snow. The sun. It's like living in a painting.

But I could live anywhere as long as it's with my wife. I love her more than I love myself, and that is something I'm working on. Our problems were never a question of love — they were a question of relationship.

I'm the type of person who likes to take care of things as they arise. If I have something to say, I'm going to say it, but my wife tends to sweep it all under the rug and turn her attention to the mountain, where she is more in tune with her place in the universe. We have vastly different methods of dealing with adversity, and there have been moments so volatile that the only thing missing was a match to send us up in flames.

We know when to tread lightly even if we don't always do it. We also know that it takes more than love for a relationship to endure. It takes faith that two people can bring out the best in each other, even when they see and feel only the worst. From the beginning, we knew we were getting the best of each other.

As heavenly as Frisco might seem, those of us who live here know how a ski season can occasionally wear on you after several months of snow, more snow, and vicious cold. In Frisco, the drudgery of shoveling is lessened by the promise that spring melt-off will leave behind countless shades of green, splashing creeks, and meadows bursting with wildflowers.

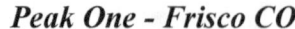

Peak One - Frisco CO

That is where my heart lies now.

I feel it's beat each time I stand atop a peak and look 360 degrees upon a snow-laced world before pointing my snowboard downhill wondering where the mountain will take me. I love the steeps, the jumps, and landings, carving turns like calligraphy. What I love most, however, is speed.

I timed myself at well over 50 miles per hour, and when you're moving that fast, even if you're not stoned, you hear the wild sounds of speed and see only what lies before you. Nothing else matters. And without even thinking about it, you learn balance.

Me Snowboarding at A-Basin on East Wall

You also learn respect, because when you forget to respect the mountain, that's when you get hurt, when you fly blind and find yourself lying alone on the snow at the base of a tree waiting for the ski patrol to haul your ass down in a sled. Its at this point in time your quick to realize. The mountain always wins.

3

GROWING UP: A BOY WITHOUT A NAME

I was born in Cleveland, Ohio, on October 10, 1960. My mother was walking down the street on a hill near our house when she slipped and fell, breaking both arms and going into labor eight weeks early. Back then, the odds of my survival were so slim, my parents were advised by the doctor not to name me. My birth certificate to this day still identifies me as Blank, Blank French. I was known as Lanny Bill until I turned twelve, when my birth certificate was amended by my mother.

My first weeks on this earth were spent in an incubator causing damage to my lungs, ears, and, most noticeably, my eyes. I was sensitive to light and blinked continuously and with unnerving exaggeration. My siblings' and their friends didn't want to be around me because I was different, and all of them called me Blinky.

Ever since I can remember, anytime my father and siblings referred to my birth, they said I wasn't born—I was hatched. I believed them all the way up until second grade when my teacher went around the room asking us for our birthdays. In front of the entire class, I said to her with a straight face that I wasn't born: I was hatched. That is what I was told and that is what I believed.

It seemed cruel that anyone, let alone my family, would lead me on like that. It was one of many childhood misgivings that alienated me and, eventually, instilled in me the belief that "I didn't matter".

Lone Boy

My mother and father had four children by the time I was born. They met in high school when Dad was a senior, and Mom was a sophomore. She was the adopted daughter of a Methodist minister and his wife, who had several miscarriages before deciding to adopt. Grandpa Ernie played a profound role in my life.

As I grew older, I confided in him that sometimes my imagination would get out of control and my dreams showed me things that I thought were crazy and that sometimes I heard "voices". He said I was lucky. "Stay close to your voices, as they will never let you down," he told me. I was less confused and afraid after that. As I look back to the days when he was alive. It seems funny that we never agreed on religion, but I always felt he respected me and my views.

Ernie was there for me in many, many ways. He even loaned me money when I needed it for college. Of which I paid every penny back as my uncle and father found out after he died when reviewing his finances. He was just a good guy, and I admired him a lot. When Grandma was sick with Alzheimer's, Grandpa Ernie took care of her for years right up to the end. He died a short time later.

I thought that the voices I heard in my head were internal. As a young boy, I spent a lot of time outside playing alone and talking to myself, but in third grade I specifically remember hearing a voice, and it wasn't mine.

The gym at my elementary school had huge glass windows on one side of the building. At the beginning of class, all the students, about 30 of us, would sit in rows across the front of the stage. We could see that it was very stormy and turning dark. I was looking outside with my buddy David, who was looking a little nervous and scared. As I looked at him, I noticed the gym teacher at the back of the stage calming students who were scared.

Just then I heard a loud voice in my head telling me to run and get out of the gym. "Let's get out of here," I screamed out. I immediately jumped up and ran to the doors. Everyone followed me, and just as we closed the doors behind us, the glass windows shattered all over the gym floor. David and I sat on the floor up against the wall shaking. We didn't know at the time that we had just survived a tornado.

The voices told me that I would be moving to a different town and attending a different school, which happened many times during my life. They told me about world events I knew nothing about.

Many times, the voices made me feel confused and afraid, but Grandpa Ernie always assured me that there was nothing wrong with me, and maybe that's all I really needed to know.

Mom was the eternal optimist and was nurturing and giving. It was never, ever about her. She would call me up on the phone and say, "Whatcha doin'?" followed quickly by, "When are you coming home?" She would tell me how much she loved me over and over. And now I wish I had told her the same.

We count on our mothers for clichés that can be drawn upon for encouragement and comfort later in life. I can still hear Mom say: "If you can dream it, you can make it happen." "One day at a time, just take life one day at a time." "Don't worry, it will be better in the morning." "You can get high. But if you stop performing and achieving or your grades start to suffer, you're done!"

Her dreams, as modest as they were, never came true. Her biggest was to find her parents. She searched for her biological mother forever and had a couple leads but never found her. Sadly, she passed over twenty-five years ago in North Carolina wondering who she was and where her family was. Before she died, she wanted all of us kids to visit, but it never happened. I gave part of the eulogy at her funeral and wrote a poem titled "We Are All Here Mom. We Are All Finally Here." Truth be told, I didn't write the poem. My voices did. It only took me a couple of hours the night before her funeral.

My dad's early years were very difficult because his father drank too much and eventually lost his business at the bottom of a bottle. His father was abusive, but Dad excelled in school and sports and was the first in his family to graduate from college. He also was a Marine and fought in the Korean War, where he was shot a couple of times and awarded the Purple Heart. My dad is a hero.

I remember him telling the story about how he once was sitting around a fire and talking to his buddies in the war zone. He looked away and when he turned back around, he saw his buddy with his head shot off. Maybe it was because he was a Marine that his expectations were so high, and maybe war and its effects caused his violent outbursts. Demons are ruthless in their pursuit of heroes.

He found that fear and intimidation were effective motivators. The first time I got the belt was when my brother and I were in the attic above my dad's bedroom, and we were being too loud. I remember Dad coming upstairs telling us to be quiet, and he had the belt. It was brutal. I'll never forget it.

He was a big man, six-foot-four, slightly balding on top. He was very athletic, smart, and could fix anything. He once rebuilt a car from the chassis on up. He knew about carpentry, science, gardening. He could look at the nighttime sky and make sense of its order. Dad seemed to have an answer to every question.

"When you do something, do it right the first time." "Always give 120 percent if you're going to do anything." "You are who you associate with."

And my personal favorite: "You take yourself with you…" Which to me meant you can run, you can move, you can start over, but you're still the same person.

His decrees come back to me time and again, and as I try to hear and recall his words, I don't remember him saying that he loved me or was proud of me. Maybe they got caught in his throat, or maybe he felt that I didn't need to hear him say them. Or even more sad, maybe I just don't remember!

The first job I remember him having was athletic director at a YMCA in Ohio, where Mom also worked managing the daycare center. He also taught and coached high school before the job at the Y. Things were very tough in the 1960s, and both of my parents had to work to make ends meet. My first memories are going to daycare with Mom when I was five. During summer breaks, Dad took me to work with him, and I could swim before the outdoor pool opened. I had the place mostly to myself, and it was soothing and calm, a perfect setting for a young imagination.

Each Christmas Mom made sure everybody got a few gifts, and I remember seeing her stress when putting presents on layaway or charging them. She took care of the bills, and when Dad got turned down on the car loan, he blamed her. He started yelling at Mom as soon as we got in the house. I was scared and ran down to the basement to hide. What I heard during those next few minutes was terrifying.

I heard my father beating my mother, flesh hitting flesh, and Mom was screaming in pain every time he struck her. I couldn't take it any longer. It was one of the first times I had heard voices. They told me to go help her, so I ran upstairs. When I got there, I found my mother on the floor on her knees in front of the sink, and Dad was getting ready to hit her again. I threw myself into him as hard as I could, and I screamed at him to stop. I was punching him in the back, and he turned and backhanded me across my face and sent me flying across the floor into the corner. I remember him looking down at me.

I kept yelling at him to stop. I was mad and scared. He looked at me and looked at my mom bleeding from her mouth and holding my head. He turned around and walked upstairs and shut himself in his bedroom. Mom got me up to make sure I was OK and thanked me for running up and helping her. She took me by the hand and got up, and we stood there and held each other. She looked like she was in a daze, and as she was looking at me, she reached over and grabbed the car keys.

"We gotta get out of here," she said. "We gotta go find your brothers and sisters and get everybody in. We're not coming home tonight." We got into the car and drove around, found everybody and spent that night with a family friend. It was a terrifying night for all of us. And my brothers and sisters— none of us talked about it. I remember all of us just sitting there, not interacting.

We went home the next day, and Dad was still in his room. We just kind of laid low. The next day, they had to go to work together at the YMCA, and Mom had bruises on her face. It was obvious what had happened, and in the next few weeks, Dad was asked to look for another YMCA. He interviewed at a couple places before accepting a job as Executive Director at a YMCA in Pittsburgh. It turned out to be a promotion.

I was twelve when we moved to a Pittsburgh suburb. It was the big city compared to our small town in Ohio, and the schools were huge. The roads were full of turns and curves around mountains, and because of that I had to look out the front window at the horizon or I would get car sick. The streets were also crowded with lots of cars, and everything took longer to get to. Instead of a two-minute walk to school, we had to ride the school bus for over an hour. Instead of a five-minute drive for dad to get to work, it took him over an hour plus on a good day.

The school I went to was very large. And it was sports that allowed me to fit in and make friends. The sixth-grade soccer coach recruited me to play on the team, which helped me meet kids. After spending so much time alone, it felt good to belong, to wear a uniform and to be counted upon, to be slapped on the back and praised. I could understand sports, with its rules and strategies, but the rest of life was confusing and, sometimes, painful.

About a year after we moved, Mom and I were sitting in the front room watching television one night when we heard the front screen door open and close. Mom got up and opened the door, and an envelope dropped to the floor. She picked it up and opened it, removing a letter and pictures. I saw a shocked look on her face, so I rushed to her. She started reading the letter and turned silent. Then she put the letter back in the envelope and went to her room.

Not a word was said to me, nothing, but I knew something was wrong. Later that week, I heard my parents talking about a woman, and my brothers told me something about Dad having an affair with his secretary. I didn't know what that meant, but everything changed after that.

Mom turned solemn and distant. I was looking for her one day because I had questions about an upcoming field trip. I looked in my parents' bedroom. The bathroom door was shut, so I knocked but there was no answer. Then I heard something, so I knocked again.

"Mom, are you in there?"

I opened the door and found her sitting on the toilet with a razor blade at her wrist. She was pressing hard against her wrist making tiny slices. She looked like she was in a trance.

"Mom, Mom what are you doing?"

She didn't move. She was staring at her wrist, and she started moving the razor back and forth. I saw blood starting to drop to the floor. I screamed at her, and I grabbed her hand and accidentally cut my fingers with the razor blade. Then she fell to the floor. She just lay there kind of in a fetal position. She screamed and started crying. I never heard her cry like that.

"He doesn't love me. He doesn't love me. He wants a divorce. He doesn't want me anymore." I sat down and held her. No one else was home. She made me promise not to tell anyone, especially Dad, so I made her that promise, but she had to promise me that she would never do anything like that ever again. It was our secret.

Mom and Dad called for a family meeting that following Sunday evening and announced that they were getting a divorce. After the announcement, we all went to our rooms. There was no discussion. I just cried. I shared a bedroom with my brothers, and they came in and told me to grow up, that they knew it was coming. They acted like it was no big deal. That night I pulled the covers over my head and just cried. I tried to be quiet because if I didn't, my brothers would beat me up. I was almost asleep when Mom came in and sat on my bed and lay down next to me and hugged me. "You can stop crying," she said. "Your father and I are going to work things out because of you. We aren't going to get a divorce because it's not fair to you."

I wasn't sure what to think, and that made me feel even worse. I began to think that I would be the one depriving them of what they truly wanted. Would there be more fights, and would they be my fault for keeping them together? If Mom tried to kill herself again, would it be my fault? Would I stand at her grave knowing that if hadn't been for me, she would still be alive?

A few weeks later, there was a second family meeting in which my parents confirmed that they were going to stay together, and it wasn't long before we were on the move again, this time to Maryland. We rented a huge farmhouse on a big lot in the middle of the country. It was beautiful, just the opposite of our home in suburban Pittsburgh.

There were a couple barns and a river that ran by the house with a swimming hole, and next to the road was a covered bridge built in the 1800s. There were no neighbors, and we could see the Chesapeake Bay from a hill next to the house. It was beautiful. I played in the woods all summer and hung out at the swimming hole and did a lot of fishing.

When school started that fall. I turned to sports again to meet friends. I loved athletics, and they provided me some measure of control over my life. The harder I practiced and the more determined I became, the better I got. And more doors opened for me. I have always been the type of person who, if I do something, I'm going to work until I'm the best at it. Sports gave me that opportunity.

Perhaps I have Dad to thank for that. Despite his occasional explosive temper and abusive behavior, his ambition and competitive nature were undeniable, and for better or for worse I share those qualities.

I know that Dad had horrible moments during the war, and he never fully escaped them, but that didn't lessen the pain he inflicted. And when I awake from nightmares, my mother's words linger in the air. To this day sometimes I feel her presence when I'm driving down the road that sends chills up my spine, and she still is telling me that things will be better by morning. Mom taught me hope, while my father taught me resolve. Both have served me well.

4

FOOTBALL

Our move to Maryland was made too late in the fall for me to play football, so I didn't get to participate in sports until the winter basketball league. My father encouraged us to participate in athletics. As head of the YMCA, he knew all the high school coaches, and it was important to him that we excel.

My oldest brother, who was destined for football stardom, quit the team his sophomore year in high school to play tennis, and Dad exploded. He told him he was throwing his future away and called him a "faggot." I don't think their relationship was ever the same after that. My dad pretty much disowned him, even though my brother went on to become a tremendous tennis player.

In high school, I received financial aid to attend a private academy, which happened to be the oldest boarding school in the country. It had only about 125 students, and among its alumni were two signers of the Declaration of Independence. It was a great school as more than 98 percent of its graduates went on to college.

There, I excelled in academics and had a very successful football career. I was all-conference in the Baltimore area both my junior and senior years. My grades were solid, and I made the National Honors Society.

The school was an awakening. There were students from all over the world. I was a day student, which meant I lived at home rather than in the dorms. As I look back, it was really a school for misfits. Some were students who struggled at home and in their local public schools. Most were very wealthy or very smart, and some (mostly the day students) were like me, just regular kids trying to make it to college and a better life than their parents.

It was during this time that my home life began to improve. I was the only one living at home with Mom and Dad. My sisters were now married and my brothers each joined the military and never returned back home. Over the years, my parents had tried to buy houses but didn't have enough money to qualify for a mortgage. In Maryland they were finally able to buy their own house. It wasn't the largest house in the neighborhood. But it was theirs and they were very proud.

The three of us seemed to grow closer. Dad, Mom and I talked about everything. We had dinner together every night, and after dinner we watched *Get Smart* or *I Dream of Jeannie* or something, the same shows every week. We had a routine, and life seemed more stable, except that after watching TV in the evening I went to my bedroom and got high.

Mom knew that I was smoking dope, but she didn't mind as long as I kept my grades up and worked hard in sports. Many times she would come to my room a couple hours before Dad got home to remind me to air out the room. At the time, I thought it was cool, but now I see that she was enabling me, allowing me to go down a road I would someday regret.

When I got my driver's license, I would drive my car to campus and pick up my buddies in the dorms and sneak out for a peek of a brand-new world. Life was changing quickly, and it was an exciting time, a stew of sports, academics, home, marijuana, alcohol, hormones, girls, and an unfulfilled need to matter or even be idolized in the way young people seek glory.

After high school graduation in 1979, I played football at a small, Division III school in Maryland. Camp started in August, and I was fit and ready when I walked onto campus after having trained hard all summer.

Camp was tough, nothing like high school, but I made my mark, and I was working with the varsity team. I was a linebacker, but I didn't really have the size for that position, so I was switched to tailback, made the varsity traveling team and even got to play in a few games my first year.

I had a great sophomore season. I was in the starting rotation, and we were nationally ranked. The season came and went, and everything was going great for me. I was in a fraternity, and my grades were good, and I was having fun.

That was until late one night when I went to visit my girlfriend after a party and found her in bed with the captain of the football team. I picked up his clothes and walked out of the room without a word. I was walking down the hallway, and she followed me screaming. She pulled me into a restroom shouting, "How could you? How could you?" Make no mistake, it was 1 a.m., and I was trashed.

She began attacking me by hitting me in the face and chest. She was wailing on me. Beating me! So, I grabbed her wrists and kept her arms apart so she couldn't hit me. Then she bit me on the wrist, and, out of reflex, I slapped her in the face. That slap changed my life.

The following Monday, I was called to the dean's office and was suspended from school. Out of college, just like that! And I couldn't go home. So, I went looking for a job and ended up working for a concrete construction crew more than an hour away in Baltimore. This event taught me humility and made me determined to return to college and redeem myself, but until then I had to earn a living. After working the winter months at the construction job, I started working as a bartender a few blocks from my place in the town next to the college.

I was determined to clear my name after the incident with my girlfriend, as my name and reputation meant everything to me. That summer, in preparation for my junior year, I worked out extremely hard and long. I ran ten to fifteen 120-meter sprints every day. I would do at least 500 pushups every day because I didn't have a weight room, and then I would go for two- to three-mile runs for endurance.

I got my weight up to more than 210-plus pounds, and when I arrived at camp that mid-August, my coaches noticed. Halfway through that camp I was nominated for captain by my peers. At the end of camp, I was selected as the most improved player on the team. I was proud, as my hard work had paid off.

Then, during a preseason game in Virginia, we had a third down and long. The quarterback called a play in which he faked to the right, while I slipped out of the backfield into the left flat.

He turned and passed it to me. I caught it and started running. Just as I was about to reach the first down marker, I lunged. My right leg was fully extended. and a defensive player hit my knee from the side. At the same time as the hit, I heard a sound that I will never forget. It sounded like 200 rubber bands snapping when stretched too tight. It was horrible. The ref blew the whistle, and my knee bent the opposite way and I instantly felt nauseous from the impact. The medical team came out to check me out, and of course I said, "I'm fine, all good." And then when I tried to stand up the leg gave out as I dropped into the medical team's arms. The Monday after the game, I went to the doctor, who said my season was finished, and I needed surgery. Once again, just like that my life changed.

Surgery went well, and after being released, I was living off-campus in a house with some fraternity brothers, and I guess it was pretty cold. College students don't like spending money on things like heat. My parents came to visit me after I got out of the hospital, and it happened to be my 21st birthday. My dad started a fire in the fireplace, and when the house warmed up, he said he smelled something rotten.

Unbeknownst to me the smell was coming from my cast, so he took a knife and poked holes through it. There were spots of blood and it smelled terrible. He asked my mom to call the doctor right away. They immediately drove me back to the hospital, where the doctor met us in the emergency room. That's when I passed out. I had gangrene, and it was very serious. The doctor told my parents we were lucky. I was within twelve hours of losing my leg and inside 24 hours of losing my life. My mom and dad visiting me on my 21st birthday saved my life. Doctors had to do several surgeries to clean out the infection.

After the first of many surgeries to remove the infection, I was in a cast, and it had a hole, a window over the infected area so they could change the dressing. One day while a nurse was cleaning the leg through the window, I asked her if I could look at my knee, and when I did, I immediately passed out.

I remember coming to and being asked how many white keys were on the piano.

"52," I said.

"How many black keys?"

"36."

Her name was Kim. She had lived at the hospital for a long time with a very rare skin disease. She was around 24 years old and had been there since she was twelve or thirteen. Her parents had brought her their many years ago and left. She had a very rare skin disease, and her skin was slowly shrinking off her body. Her eyelids were gone, her lips and ears were gone, and her skin was stretched so tight, it tore.

I remember my first encounter with her as I walked around the hospital the day before my original surgery. At the end of the hall my room was on were several signs informing you to stop, do not enter, private area. Another sign read only authorized staff allowed beyond this point. I was like, wow, what's this all about.

So, me being me I quietly went by the sign and peaked into the room the signs were outside. As I peaked in, I spotted a person sitting by the window. And in the reflection of the window, I could see a face that didn't look like anything that I had ever seen. The skin was stretched tight, the person had no nose, ears or hair, and I immediately turned and ran out.

To my surprise, her sweet voice was there after every one of the four surgeries. She held my hand and would tell me everything was going to be OK, and she gave me riddles to take my mind off the pain and nausea. She was a beautiful spirit, and we were buddies.

I will never forget her. I had such a great life compared to her, and she never complained. Instead, she tried to make life better for others, even for people she didn't know. When I was sick and vomiting from the anesthesia, she was there to hold my hand. I often think of her kindness and wisdom to this day.

I went into the hospital thinking that my knee was the only thing in need of repair, but sometimes you don't know something is broken until its fixed.

I left Johns Hopkins knowing that in the midst of sickness and bereavement, there was grace and true selflessness in the world sent by angels that come to us and give us faith and hope. And that was truly healing.

I was in the hospital for over three months. I arrived weighing 215 pounds, and I left only weighing 149. When I went back to the doctor to see how I was doing after all the surgeries, I was told that I could play football again, but I would have to wear a brace on my knee. There's no way I would do that, so I quit the team, which meant I had no way of paying for college. I decided to enroll in ROTC for the financial aid and was tentatively accepted pending testing.

Everything crashed in on me again later that school year when I was suspended for a second time. I had to take a Spanish class to fulfill my graduation requirements, and we had a big test coming up. The fraternity I was in kept copies of tests from different professors and different years. It was all over campus that there was a copy of the test we were going to take. I wanted to pass on my own, and I did, but I was called into the dean's office the next day.

He asked if I knew about the test being available. I told him I knew about it. Everybody on campus knew about it. I explained to him that I didn't cheat, and he said that the professor could tell that I didn't cheat. After the ten-minute conversation, he told me I was free to leave his office. The next day, I received a letter stating I was suspended because, even though I didn't cheat, I didn't report to the honor society that a test was available to students.

I had lost football and was suspended twice. I had a reputation as an abuser and cheater, even though I was neither. And now, college was gone. My life was again in turmoil.

But at times like that, I think about how many black keys and white keys are on a piano, and something about that gives me hope that everything will turn out fine. I went to see Kim a few different times after my hospital visit. By the last time I visited she wasn't allowed to have visitors. When I approached her room, I once again read all of the signs that were there the first time, I saw her. Unlike that first time, a nurse noticed me and quickly ran down the hall to stop me. But inside the room Kim heard the nurse and my voice. When she heard my voice, she yelled out to the nurse to let me in. When I walked in all I could see was her smile and her arm reaching out for my hand. By this time her legs had been amputated, her fingers were gone, and her skin was stretched tighter than ever, but she could still smile. And she did, when she saw me walk into her room.

The next time I went to see her a couple of years later, her room she lived in for over fifteen years was empty, and she was gone.

I hope somebody was holding her hand.

Me Playing Rugby and Running Through the Defense

5

RUGBY

After my second suspension, I went to work at a catering hall, one of the biggest on the East Coast and I managed my own event room, making sure everything got done. Famous people from all over the country would come for meetings, weddings or other events. I prepared a room once for President George H.W. Bush. He had Secret Service agents all over, and they gave me clearance so I could make sure everything was taken care of. It was a great job. It was challenging and interesting, and I loved it.

I made very good money, and the general manager called me his star. Over one-and-a-half years, I managed nearly a hundred weddings. I saved money to go back to college and moved to an area just north of Baltimore where I met up with an old fraternity brother working as a bartender. He got me a job tending bar with him, and I quit my job as a catering manager.

It was 1985, I had saved enough money to enroll back in college. Working at the bar didn't pay much, especially when back then you could buy a beer for 45 cents. The place was a classic Baltimore local's bar. Everybody knew everybody and everybody's business.

One of my roomies was a rugby player, and he was always trying to get me to play, but I always said I wasn't interested. And that the game looked very dangerous. Then one day he asked me to go for a jog with him. I told him I still wasn't interested in that crazy sport, but he kept saying that I had been inside all day and needed to get out for a while. We went for a jog and unbeknownst to me, he ran me over to his team's rugby training.

There I was. I told him I would give it a try, and it didn't take long to fall in love with the sport. I played my first match when I was 24 years old and scored several times. The next match I had even more success. Rugby in 1984 was a niche sport played as a club sport by guys who weren't really athletically trained, but they were tough and dedicated. They also wanted to have fun and party, so, in most ways, I was well suited.

Rugby is a violent game of intelligence, fitness, execution, teamwork and tradition, many of the latter involving song and beer. It's known as a gentleman's game, but it is played in spit and blood. It's not unlike going to battle, which results in the unique kinship among survivors that transcends generations. We become family and feel a bond rarely found in life. Where we all have a place at the table.

In 1994, our rugby team went undefeated and qualified for the national championships held over Memorial Day weekend in Austin, Texas. We were playing the national powerhouse, a team from San Diego. We were the underdogs, and nobody gave us a chance. Sports Illustrated even did an expose on the California team because this would be an unprecedented victory if they were to win this championship again.

Prior to the match, we all had ten minutes to individually get ourselves ready. I was at the end of the pitch behind the goal posts, and I was jumping up and down, springing higher and higher with every jump. I came to tears thinking about all the people who got me to this great day: coaches, players who had passed, players who taught me things and took me under their wings, my father, and my wife sacrificing the time I spent preparing and playing matches over the past twelve years.

My emotions were huge. I heard voices tell me that this was what it was all about: challenges, memories, appreciation, gratitude, sacrifices, respect, honor, on and on. It was a moving ten minutes, and it had as much to do with life as it did with sport.

The match was incredible. I had arguably my best performance on a rugby pitch ever, despite playing with a hand I had broken early in the second half. When the final whistle blew, and we had won. Me and my teammates knew that all the hard work had paid off. It was one of the happiest moments of my life.

What made it even more special was that there had never been an East Coast team that had won the National Championship. All the previous championships had been being won by West Coast teams like the one from San Diego, the team we just defeated for the title.

It was a great time in my life. I was married and in love. I was moving up the career ladder after years of tending bar.

And we were the champs.

Not that there's anything wrong with being a bartender.

One thing about bars is that you never know who is going to walk through the door and change your life.

On a Friday night in 1985, a guy came in sat at the bar and started asking me about my job, my life, and my history. We chatted, I sold him a couple shots, and every time I asked him if he wanted to buy something, he did. I even sold him dessert, and no one buys dessert in a local bar.

Later in the evening, he asked if I had ever thought about going into sales. He owned a company that sold high tech telephone systems, and he told me to call him if I was interested in a sales job, but he said before he would interview me, I had to read a book, *Think and Grow Rich.*

I never have been much of a reader, but I went and got the book. It turned out I had been living the theme of the book all my life. Its message was that if you could think of it and keep it in your mind, you could make it happen. My mother told me the same thing. This was another turning point in my life.

A couple months later, I met this other guy who owned a copier company. He gave me a better job working with his young company. I did very well selling copiers, and I really liked my bosses. The regional director of the company who traveled the whole country took me under his wing and taught me a lot about management and sales and sales techniques.

A year and a half later, a head hunter who was the wife of a rugby mate recruited me for another new and even better sales job. She said she was very impressed with my track record in sales and had a job available selling for a huge payroll company. They were world-renowned, and I was soon making more money than I had ever made.

I did so well that I decided against going back to college. I stopped 15 credits short of getting my degree, but I didn't care. I was making good coin. After a year with the payroll company, I achieved the company's highest sales award.

A year or so later another opportunity presented itself when I was approached by a rugby old boy from my club who was the orthopedic surgeon for the U.S. National Rugby Team called the Eagles. We started talking, and he said he was going to open a bar in Baltimore—a rugby bar. He asked me if I was interested in helping him and be his bar manager, and, possibly, part owner.

I decided to take the job, and when I told my general manager at the payroll company of my decision, he called me a unicorn and said I was making a huge mistake and would never be able to go back to the corporate world, but I decided to take the risk and go for a dream. That dream turned out to be my wife.

Rugby Team Jerseys Post Match

6

OUR LOVE STORY

The first time I saw her it was 1992, when she came to my bar with a friend who was dating a rugby player.

Her buddies would tell her, "Stay away, don't mess with that guy." I guess I had a reputation.

I asked her out, and of course she turned me down. Then one day my boss asked her if she would be interested in volunteering to hand out fliers, because we were trying to generate some lunch business. I was supposed to meet her at 10:30 a.m. at the bar to help her, but I rolled in around noon, and she was pissed. "Where have you been?"

I explained that I also ran a deli, and there were some problems that made me late. I told her we should meet at 10:30 the next day, but she said, "What are you doing now?" I told her I had paperwork to do, then I was going on a bike ride. When I came down after doing the paperwork, she was still there.

"Can I come with you?"

"I said sure, if you want to."

We went to her apartment downtown to get her bicycle, and then we drove out to my place just outside the city line of Baltimore to pick up my bike. When we arrived at the location, we would be bike riding. We unloaded our bikes, and I started out toward the biking trails. We rode about a quarter mile on the road, then I turned off the road onto a bike trail. I continued a little way down the off-road bike trail before I looked behind me and she was not there, so I circled back to find her. She was still up on the road. She did not know we were going off-road mountain biking. She thought we were going road biking.

She was dressed all in white. We jumped on the trail and 45 minutes later, she was covered in mud. She was just filthy. And all I could see was her huge, beautiful smile. We were riding next to a reservoir, and the trail was really wet. We stopped at a place next to the reservoir called Sam's Point. Sam was a dog who was buried there many years before. There was a small headstone placed there by his owner. And there were always a couple of lacrosse balls next to his headstone because he must of loved playing with them.

We were sitting there chatting. She was standing against a tree talking to me, and I was down by the lake. I looked up at her, but she didn't know I was looking. She was beautiful. I remember that exact moment when I knew she was the one. She was standing under a tree with her arms above her head against a low hanging branch as she slowly swayed back and forth under the limb. Her smile was so beautiful and that's when it hit me. She is the one!

On the way home, I was getting ready to drop her off, and we both said at the same time, "What are you doing tomorrow?"

Some guys would suggest a fancy—but not too fancy—restaurant suited for quiet conversation and expensive wine. Not me. I suggested a baseball game. And she said yes. We went to watch the Orioles play at Camden Yards. A beer, some popcorn and peanuts, a lovely companion, and baseball. We cheered for the Orioles, and the more we learned about each other, the more we wanted to be together.

A few weeks later. My rugby club played in an annual Labor Day tournament on a beach in Delaware. It was a long weekend, and when I wasn't playing in a match, we were in bed making love, talking, and laughing. We met up with our friends at the bar, but other than that it was just the two of us.

The weekend went quickly. I dropped her off at her apartment after the drive back from the beach, went home, and flopped down on my couch. After about an hour, there was a knock on the door. It was late, and I was wondering who it might be. I turned on the porch light, and there she stood, wearing a knee-length raincoat. She stood there with a big beautiful smile and opened her raincoat, and all she was wearing was sexy underwear. I opened the door, gave her a huge hug and kiss, and took her to my bedroom. We have never been apart since that weekend.

Less than a year after we met, I decided to propose. We were in Ocean City, Maryland, on a Saturday night. The day before, I had gone shopping for a ring, but I had one problem: I didn't have any money, certainly not enough to buy her the ring I wanted to give her, but I said "Fuck it" and went into a little jewelry store and spent less than $100 on a ring. If she loved me, the size of the ring shouldn't matter. That's what every broke guy tells himself in a jewelry store.

I arrived that Friday evening at her place where she was staying with a friend and the next day, we went to the beach.

We had dinner reservations for 7 p.m. So after a day at the beach we went to our place to get cleaned up. I was feeling nervous and excited. I didn't have any special plans other than getting on my knee to propose. We both jumped in the shower, and she washed my back. I washed hers, and we stood there chatting, hugging, and kissing. She suddenly stopped and stepped back to say, "I have something to ask you."

"Ask away," I said.

She asked me to marry her, and I nearly passed out. She repeated, "Will you marry me?" I was floored.

"Of course, I will. Yes, I'll marry you."

Then I told her, "You're not going to believe this." I jumped out of the shower to grab the ring then ran back into the shower. "I was going to ask you to marry me tonight at dinner."

There we were in the shower. I had just said yes. She opened the box with the little ring and said, "Yes, I'll marry you." We were in tune in a way that was intoxicating. We wanted more and more of each other. And we had the rest of our lives to make that happen.

We started planning our wedding on the way home from the beach. We decided to elope in Jamaica the following Thanksgiving Day, 1993. We had to spend five days on the island before our marriage could become legal. So we invited some friends to join us for a vacation and our wedding.

On the day we were married, the weather was beautiful. We gathered at the beach near sunset. I was wearing white cotton pants, a blue silk shirt, bare feet, and a huge smile. She wore a beautiful white lace dress and was carrying a huge bouquet of flowers that her friends had made for her that day.

Wedding Day Sunset in Jamaica

She came up to me, we hugged, we kissed, stood there facing each other, staring into each other's eyes. It was truly magical. After the brief ceremony, our officiant pronounced us husband and wife, and then we kissed.

After the ceremony, we all went back to our beach house, where the resort team had prepared a steak and lobster dinner. We all sat around a large table in the main room and had a great wedding feast before we cut the cake and slammed it into each other's mouths, making a perfect mess on our faces.

We knew a reggae band was playing nearby that night, so we headed there to hear music. It was getting late, and the bar was starting to close, and, unbeknownst to us, my wife's brother had paid the band to follow us to our beach shack and continue playing.

When we got back to where we were all staying, we had our first dance to the song, "One Love." We later snuck out to our honeymoon suite, and we heard the band repeating the song.

It was a mesmerizing journey of spirits—a joining of spirits.

7

ATLANTA AND BACK

Six years after our marriage, in 1999, I was hired for a job that allowed me to work virtually for a time management company. I was on the education team for sixteen years before, on my 55th birthday, I got a call saying they were downsizing. I was ten years away from retirement, and they were laying me off.

It was devastating. I had to reinvent myself, but two months later I had another job. On my wife's 50th birthday, we were celebrating at a bed and breakfast, and I got there late. My wife knew I had a late interview that day so when I walked in, she yelled, "Did you get the job?" It got kind of quiet.

"Yes, I got the job." But, I told her there was one catch.

"We have to move to Atlanta."

"Alabama?" she said.

"No, Atlanta." I replied.

"Where's Atlanta? She asked.

To Atlanta

Prior to accepting the offer, I had reached an agreement with the company that would allow me to return to Colorado if I hit my goals for that year. They accepted my request. I moved there in January of 2016, and my wife joined me in Atlanta later in May after ski season.

I worked my tail off to make it happen, and my boss made good on his deal and allowed me to return to Colorado. It was the Wednesday before Thanksgiving weekend when I was told I could move back home. The day after Thanksgiving I went to work, and when I came home, my wife had packed everything up in boxes and was ready to move. Our lease went to February, but it didn't matter. We packed up and we moved as fast as we could. We were back in Colorado by the first of December.

Back to Colorado

Our main house is in Evergreen located in the front range just west of Denver. We call it the Ponderosa. We had rented it out when we moved to Atlanta, so when we returned, we lived in a small condo we owned in Frisco. One of my wife's friends was living with us at the time, and it was just too small for us, so we looked to buy a bigger place.

We found a house and decided to remodel, expand, and build an apartment underneath. My wife was overseeing the project, because I had to work, and it turned out to be a series of problems with the framers, who, we later learned, were not building according to the architect's plans. They were ordering materials they didn't need, and the entire summer was chaos. And that led to problems in our marriage.

Finally, when construction was in its final stages, late August/early September 2017, the work crew asked for several days off to go hunting. When my wife came to me to talk about it, I kind of lost it with her. I explained that they were misleading us and not working to the architect's plans, and then on top of that they wanted time off to go hunting.

That was way too much for me. I couldn't understand it. It was like they had brainwashed my wife, and she wasn't hearing anything I was saying. She was asking to give them time off, and I became angry. I got louder and louder because she just couldn't hear me.

The House Project Before

I had to get out of the house, so I called our dog Kimba, and grabbed his leash. I needed to go for a walk, as I was furious, at wit's end. Kimba and I walked across town, and he could sense that I was upset. Kimba's very sensitive to anyone's feelings and emotions. I could see he was sad, so I tried to change my demeanor, lighten up to cheer him up, but I couldn't get myself to relax. We went on one of our usual hikes and as we went up the mountain looking down on Frisco, he just stopped and sat in the middle of the trail and wouldn't budge. I turned around to face him and squatted down. He had his head down and wouldn't come to me.

I told him, "It's OK buddy, no worries," and smiled at him. He lifted his head and sprinted right at me. He ran full speed right into me. He slammed his block head right into the middle of my chest and hit me so hard, I flew backwards onto my back.

"What was that all about, Kimba?"

Kimba on top of Peak 1

And there he stood over me panting as if saying, "I'm sorry. I didn't mean to do that!" He looked at me and immediately started licking me on the face. I needed that, thank you Kimba! I needed to get myself back under control by the time I got back to the house. The project was nearly done and somehow my wife and I needed to work together to get it finished.

I was hearing myself say: "Just relax it's the builders. Don't worry about your marriage. You guys are going to be fine." I was hearing my own self telling me to calm down.

When I returned, one of the framers came up to me. He knew I was pissed and said he was sorry, and they would get back to work immediately so we could finish the project. Then on the Friday before the final inspection, the contractors asked for their final check.

I said no we won't pay you until after the inspection. This upset my wife as they said they needed the money. So, I gave in to my wife, and we paid them. Not only that, she wanted to give them a $2,000 bonus. That led to another argument, and just to get this over, I agreed to give them the bonus. On Monday the inspector came, and after two hours told us that our project failed. There were eight areas that didn't meet code. Eight!

I immediately told my wife to call the bank and cancel the checks. It was too late. The checks were cashed last week on Friday afternoon.

We estimated that it would take somewhere between $10,000 and $15,000 to fix the problems. By then, my wife and I had completely shut down. We weren't talking. I felt betrayed by her and very alone. She felt the same way. So, there we were. The project was a mess, the relationship was even a bigger mess, and neither of us had any love we could give to each other or ourselves. I would, as usual, get high every day and just check out. There was a wedge between us, and something needed to happen to get us back on track.

House Project Completed

Twenty-plus years of anything is a long time. In our marriage we have had to move forward many times, sometimes at a crawl, sometimes blindly. In that way, we were strong. After we were married in 1993, we tried to start a family. We both wanted a large family. It's how we envisioned our lives would be and for four years we tried every different form of infertility treatment that was available. Nothing worked!! We failed and never had children, but we had to move forward. And we did. We always have.

This time was different, however. The construction project took our relationship to new depths. We were constantly fighting. Then there would be silence, and that was probably worst of all. It felt like no amount of talk would bring us back together.

I heard her tell someone that we both thought our marriage was truly over, and we needed help. At the same time, I was having serious nightmares. One in particular started shortly after I lost my job. After the project failed to pass inspection, I was having them all the time.

In the dream I was being held down with my mouth covered, and I would lay there struggling. I felt arms around my chest like someone was holding me down, and I couldn't shout for help, and as I fought to be free, I would roll all over the bed.

It would go on for several minutes, and it would wake my wife up. I was sweaty, I was fighting. I can remember coming out of those dreams and feeling terrified. Not only were the days stressful, but the nights were terrifying and horrific.

It was at that point that my wife got on the computer and Googled "marriage counseling." She scrolled down until she found a place in Sedona offering a four-day retreat for couples.

We signed up and made an appointment with an angel.

8

THE DEAL

I returned home from a week-long convention in San Francisco on Friday May 4, 2018 and was sick all weekend. I was in zombie mode, and I had another nightmare. The week before had been very, very strange, and the only time I was OK was on the convention floor. Then Monday came, and we had a telephone conversation with our angel.

"Angel" is the term used to identify the person who arranges the agenda over the four-day retreat. It was a month before our trip, so we spoke to him so he could explain how the program worked.

I told him about losing my job and moving to Atlanta and how my wife wasn't hearing me. I told him about moving back to Colorado and how we sold the condo to buy a larger house. I told him about the construction project and how it really went wrong, and how I felt alone with a wife who betrayed me and didn't hear me.

"Whatever it takes, I'll do it," I told him. "Whatever you think might work for us, I'm ready."

He explained the schedule for each day and a little bit about the experts and what their backgrounds were. Then he said he expected us both to come to Sedona sober and suggested we stop everything—drinking, smoking pot, drugs, whatever—right away.

My wife looked at me, and I looked at her. She expected me to say something, but I didn't say a word. The date of our adventure was four weeks away, and I was thinking, "Four weeks? How can I last four weeks? I have been getting high forever. Four weeks, really?"

Without missing a beat, our angel told a story about a psychiatrist in a prison mental ward in Hawaii. Without even seeing patients, he would review their files and say a Hawaiian prayer known as ho'oponopono: "I'm sorry. Please forgive me. Thank you. I love you."

Hawaii Sunset

By repeating the prayer as he held the patients' files, he healed all of them. All of them!

That afternoon I started reciting the prayer almost nonstop and immediately felt better. I felt different—at peace. It was amazing. I said it over and over: "I'm sorry. Please forgive me. Thank you. I love you." The more I said it, the more I wanted to say it.

I would think about my father. "I'm sorry Dad for what I did. Please forgive me for disappointing you and thank you for forgiving me. I love you, Dad."

"I'm sorry Dad that you had to see me and my brother smoking dope outside that bar one Christmas. Forgive me. It was totally uncool and thank you for forgiving me, and I love you, Dad."

I started remembering all the times I did something bad to friends, family, and strangers. Memories were flooding through my mind, and I just kept saying the prayer over and over and over. The next morning, I woke up feeling much better and the prayer became an important part of my daily life.

The day after speaking with the angel, I was taking Kimba for a walk. Kimba is my best friend. From the time I was a child, I have felt a special bond with dogs. Maybe it was because I was a loner and people made fun of me that I sought friendship and affection from dogs. They accept me and love me as I love them.

My wife had taken me to a farm that had lab puppies for my 50th birthday. We had lost our black lab, Jesse, about six months earlier, so we went to this farm to find a puppy, and it was Kimba who ended up finding me. I sat there watching the litter of puppies running around and playing, jumping, and bouncing off each other; all the while this little block headed lab came up to me and quietly snuck in behind my ankles and laid down under me. We sat there together for quite a while until my wife came back.

"Have you found one yet? Which one did you choose?"

"This one right here." I replied.

"This little guy right here under my legs."

He was sitting behind my feet—a little yellow lab with a block head, golden eyes, and a pink nose. He is the one. He had chosen me.

Kimba at 8 Weeks Old

Kimba and I go for hikes every day. Our routine is to walk down the street and make a left at the T intersection, walk to the park across the bridge, then through what's called the duck area and back to our house.

The day after our conversation with our angel, I decided to catch a quick little buzz. I hadn't gotten high since the Friday I left the convention, but before taking a walk with Kimba, I stepped into the garage, which we called the locker room, and had a couple small puffs.

I did those two hits, and slowly went into a strange, zombie like type of trance. I again started saying the prayer and remembered things I had totally forgotten. I started having a complete out-of-body experience. What was happening to me?

I put the leash on Kimba, and I never put him on a leash. He normally just walks beside me. I started remembering things that I had done to people, and that's when I started to hear voices. Kimba and I started on our walk and for some reason, I turned on the first road on the right. We never walk down that road, or that direction. I was falling deeper and deeper into a trance.

The voices continued to speak out to me. And I spoke back to them. I was literally walking down the street having a conversation with someone out loud:

"Who are you?

Who's talking to me?

What do you want?"

I was walking down that street now in a complete daze. Kimba was leading me. I think he knew what was going on. The voices said:

"We are here to talk about getting high, your life, your marriage. We're here for you to start talking to us again. We want to help you. You must listen to us.

I thought, *What?* Immediately I thought I was going crazy.

"We need you to listen to us, as we have always been talking to you, but because of your smoking marijuana, you haven't heard us for a very long time."

I was walking very, very slowly now and in a complete daze.

I said, "You have been with me? What? Really?"

I thought that I was losing it. I stopped and paused, and the voices continued, "We have always been here to keep you safe. We have been with you all your life, since Day One when you were born. When your mother fell."

Then they said, "Remember the 13 Cornices?"

"The Cornices?"

"We had you!"

The 13 Cornices are ski runs located in some of the steepest, most dangerous terrain on the mountain at Arapahoe Basin. I had snowboarded the Cornices hundreds of times, which is how stories about death experiences on the slopes usually begin.

My wife and I had just returned from a Hawaiian vacation, and there was a good sixteen inches of fresh new snow at A-Basin. So, my wife and a good friend of ours, Scott, all decided we couldn't pass it up. When we first got there, it was beautiful. It was a Friday afternoon, the snow was deep, the POW POW was so fluffy, and there was no crowd. We went up and did our normal warm up. A nice, casual run down to the Pali chair. Then when we got back up to the top of the lift, my wife looked at the two of us and said.

A Basin - Picture from road of 13-Cornices

"Ok, I can see that look in your eyes. I think it would probably be a good idea if you two went and had your fun, and I'll meet you in a couple hours."

Scott and I immediately headed toward the Cornices. A little way down the mountain, Scott turned right to check out another run, but I yelled at him to come back so we could go straight to the Cornices. I headed to the first drop off to make a left turn like the hundreds of times I had done this run before. And to my surprise, the powder pillow gave way. Instantly I was lying at the base of a tree. The pillow couldn't hold my board. I had no time to react. I dropped fifteen feet over the cliff. When I landed my board wrapped around a tree, and as it snapped back, my right ankle and leg exploded.

The voice reminded me of that day, how I lay there alone, broken and high in the snow, while Scott went down to get help. The board, despite shattering my body, may have saved my life by breaking my fall. Skiers and snowboarders die all the time from less.

But it wasn't the board that saved me. The voices were telling me they were with me that day. And they saved me! I didn't know what to think. I started to weep as the voice kept speaking.

"You must stop smoking pot immediately. Now, today!"

I kept thinking that I was going crazy. What was happening to me? Is this real?

The voice continued, "Yes, I'm real. We're real, you're real, and this deal is real. If you stop smoking dope, we will help you get your life back, your wife back, and we will be there to protect you and take care of you."

Kimba and I kept walking until we were in the woods behind our house, where I stopped, looked up and said, "You're making a deal with me?"

"Yes, and you need to take this deal. If you do, your life will change." I stood there silently in shock for two or three minutes.

Then I looked up and said,

"OK, done. I will take your deal!"

I haven't gotten high since that walk.

It was still about three weeks until Sedona, but my mental state had changed to a new awareness. I came back to life and was clear about everything that was going on. My thoughts started to feel clearer, and I continued to recite the prayer.

I tried to remember every little event in my life that I could apply that prayer to, everything I had done wrong to people, some of whom I hadn't spoken to in years, friends who didn't even know I had done something wrong to them.

The three weeks before leaving for Sedona went very quickly. My wife and I were getting along so much better, and even more surprising, I didn't even think about pot. It was as if I had never smoked it. I was determined to make good on my deal. Everything I needed and wanted from life hinged on it.

9

SEDONA

On Thursday, May 24, 2018, we left for Sedona via Taos, New Mexico. Taos was beautiful. It was in full bloom, and we walked around and had a nice dinner. It felt good to have hope, and we were anxious and excited to see what adventures awaited us.

Upon arrival in Sedona the next day, we checked into our hotel, then met with our angel. He asked how things had been, and we went over the last few weeks and told him we were surprised that things were going so well for us. He gave us a binder with an agenda for the next four days and asked if we had any questions. We told him we didn't, but we repeated our willingness to do whatever it took to get our lives back. Willingness was all we had.

Beautiful scenery in Sedona

In our first session, we met an incredible woman who examined our enneagrams, which analyze the influences your developmental years have on you and how that affects how you communicate and deal with others now. Very cool, we thought. My wife was a seven, which is described as an enthusiast. Enthusiasts are versatile, optimistic. They're adventurous and spontaneous. They're playful, high spirited, and practical. They can also be overextended, scattered, and undisciplined. That was her.

Enthusiasts are said to constantly seek new and exciting experiences. At their best, they are healthy, focused, and they concentrate their talents on others, on the world, and on worthwhile goals. They are highly accomplished and full of gratitude. Their basic fear is being deprived, trapped, and in pain.

I was an eight, described as being a challenger. Eights are self-confident, strong, assertive, protective, resourceful, decisive. They can also be proud and domineering. They typically have problems being close to others, which is me. At their best, Eights are self-mastering. They use their strengths to improve others' lives. They become heroic, magnanimous, and sometimes historically great. The world is an unjust place. I protect the innocent. My basic fear? Being controlled and overpowered. My enlightened virtue is innocence. All those things describe me perfectly.

We learned that sevens and eights are wingmen to each other, and together they are able to balance each other's weaknesses as we grow from each other's strengths.

The two-hour session was incredible, as we started to learn about each other and what makes us act the way we do. It was somewhat of a baseline to see where we were in our marriage and how we could move forward. It provided context for the problems we faced and tools to use in addressing them.

After lunch, we headed to our next session, which was conducted by two counselors who had been doing this work for more than 25 years. They were a husband-wife team who happened to be the parents of our angel.

The session was titled, "Renew and Refresh Your Relationship." It began with each of us spending time describing our childhoods all the way to our present state— what our lives were like, what our parents were like, what growing up was like, in essence giving an overview of our lives.

My wife went first. We talked about the good and the bad for the next two and a half hours. Our counselors had us do exercises that showed us how all people see things differently.

It was during this exercise that I had a total mental block and had to leave the room, as I couldn't remember the steps of the exercises, which were intended to help us communicate more effectively during confrontations. It's a way for the person who's unhappy to say to the other person, "Hey, look, we need to talk about this, and can we talk about this through a step-by-step process?" It allows the person to express unhappiness. And then the person who acted incorrectly shows empathy and compassion. It was a great exercise.

If I was doing something my wife didn't like, for example, my wife would say, "Lance I'm having issues with how you acted."

I should reply, "Oh, I understand. I hear you. Are you telling me that this is what makes you unhappy?"

And she would say, "Yes, this makes me unhappy."

Then I was supposed to say something like, "Oh, I understand how that could make you feel."

And she would say, "Yes, that's how it makes me feel."

"I apologize. I'm sorry I did something that made you feel like that, and I will work to not do that again. I apologize."

It was a basic empathy exercise, but it wasn't the exercise that caused my anxiety. It was me getting into my own head and losing perspective of what the exercise was, so I had to step out of the room. I started to shut down. The counselors allowed me to go outside, so I went out to the backyard, and one of them followed me and sat with me. She was holding my hand as I cried in confusion.

I was trying to get myself together. She was so kind and warm to me, and she said she understood my pain, and all I needed to do was relax. I was kind of amped up, very emotional, and it was all about, as she said, stepping out of my ego. In twenty minutes, I was able to return to the exercise.

We finished Day One, and what a day it was. My wife and I felt closer, as we started to forget ourselves and think about each other. We talked, and we actually held hands. It was an incredible afternoon.

That night, however, I had a nightmare. I felt I was stuck in a tunnel, and I was looking through the tunnel into our house, the house we had just remodeled. I was looking through a peep hole and saw a lion laying down. He jumped at me but couldn't reach me through the peephole.

My thrashing woke up my wife, and after I told her about the nightmare, I slowly came out of it, and we talked a bit and turned off the lights to get some sleep. Minutes later, she became restless and started to chat again. She woke me up, and we both laughed.

We wear night guards at night, and in order to talk, you have to take them out of your mouth. I could hear her rustling about, and I heard her take her mouthpiece out, and it became kind of funny. We started referring to our mouth pieces as seat belts. We were having fun together and laughing.

It was a small moment, but also a huge moment, and it felt like we were holding hands for the first time.

The Shaman

The next morning, we woke up at our usual time, 7 a.m. We had breakfast and got ready for our next session. Day Two started at 8:30 a.m., allowing just enough time to hit the pool, and it felt good to get in a swim. There was a hot tub there, and it was a great way to begin the day.

For Day Two, we were to meet a shaman. I had heard of shamans, but I'd never met one. We were both excited. We met up with him, and he gave us a rundown of our morning. He said we were going on a hike up a dry riverbed to talk about our lives. We would be participating in a ritual to rid ourselves of painful memories.

Being in Sedona and in the desert, I saw no reason to wear shoes, so I was barefoot, as was the shaman. We started walking on the dry riverbed, and as we walked, he told us about himself. He was in his late 60s, but he looked like he was 35. He had lived by himself for fifteen years in the Northwest wilderness. One of the issues he faced was being sexually abused by family members at a young age.

Several events in his life challenged his faith in God and man, he said. He had been counseling others for ten years, taking people up this same riverbed and doing the same exercises. "Please don't be scared, ashamed, or embarrassed to say anything on this walk," he said. "Our goal is to take anything you are hiding, holding, or have forgotten and to let it go." He had us draw a circle on a piece of paper, and inside that circle we wrote the names of our primary care givers when we were children.

My wife and I both wrote down our mom and dad. Then he had us draw a big circle with a line down the middle. On the right side we wrote the good things we remembered about our childhoods and about the people who raised us.

My wife wrote down things like loving, caring, giving to others and hard working. They gave to others and never argued. They were fun. I wrote down hard-working, nurturing, kind, smart, athletic, loving.

Then he had us fill out the other side of the circle with things that were bad. My wife wrote that her parents ignored her, shamed her, and told her that children should be seen and not heard. She felt manipulated and controlled. People would use the phrase, "That's just her." They were unsupportive, and then the shaman asked, "How does this make you feel?" She said, "I feel that something is wrong with me, and no one is telling me what it is." I wrote down abused, misled, and that I felt unworthy, and I have no value. And again, the shaman asked, "How does this make you feel?" I said that I am not worth anything, that I have no value, and that everything is my fault.

We looked at each other and at our papers, and that's when the shaman said, "Enough. Let's do an exercise to let go of all that." He told me to pick up a rock, and there were a lot of rocks in that riverbed, and throw it down as hard as I could.

"When you pick up the rock, I want you to throw it to the ground and tell that person what you thought about what they did to you," he said. "Throw that rock as hard as possible and shatter it, and let it go."

I picked up the biggest rock I could and lifted it above my head and screamed, "Stop beating my mother," and I crashed the rock down and it exploded. I got another rock and let go of the memory of catching my mom trying to commit suicide, another rock for me being the reason they didn't get divorced.

Each rock released me from the shadows. For an hour, we broke rocks. Then the shaman asked if I had any more, and I said, "I have one more." I picked up a big rock, and I threw it down on the ground. It was the one that I had to let go of. It was a huge rock, and I crushed it and screamed, "How dare you lock me in a room and jerk off in front of me." When I said that, my wife looked at me and asked, "What?"

I said it happened in Pittsburgh: someone had me in a room and locked the door and masturbated in front of me like I was nothing. I didn't even know what he was doing. But regardless, it made me feel worthless and alone. I never told anyone.

That's when the shaman spoke up: "Lance, you are important, you are worthy. Change your thoughts, change your life." To my wife, he said, "Stop questioning yourself. You are fine. There is nothing wrong with you that someone is not telling you about."

We were kind of smiling and talking to each other, and the shaman said, "You did great. You released a lot of things. You said some things that each of you had never heard before. You understand now that things that you've been holding in, you've let them go. You've crushed the rocks. They are gone. Now you need to change your thoughts, your ways of thinking, let the old ways go."

The guy was unbelievable. After we dropped him off, we both had huge smiles. We were so excited that we had revealed our core wounds. I said "fuck you" to everyone who had abused me. I was beat up by my brother from the time I was twelve until I was fourteen, and I was able to let that go.

After the session, we had time for a quick lunch before our individual sessions in the afternoon with counselors. My wife's session was titled, "Release the Anger and Resentment," and my session was titled, "Release the Toxic Thinking."

The counselor and I started talking about real-life conflicts based on scenarios that allowed me to project how I would interpret situations or conversations. We did some role-playing, and I learned that when confronted with conflict, toxic thinking took over. I needed to step back and get out of my own head. My ego is strong, so in certain scenarios, I need to back up and ask questions to make sure it's not my ego taking over.

I realized it was me who was having the bigger issues. I was blaming it on my wife when it was actually me who, because of ego, wasn't listening. This was truly an ah-ha moment for me, and it helped me understand my role in the conflicts we were having. This session was important and timed perfectly, continuing to build on our three previous sessions. I knew this realization would change our marriage. I knew what I had to work on, and I was being given the tools to help me.

When I drove back from the session to meet my wife, she instantly began to talk about her experience. I listened and told her that I understood why she was mad and angry with me for checking out and that I was finished with pot and that I would do whatever it took to be better. I told her how I had learned that my actions and toxic thoughts were being managed by my ego—my inner child—behavior driven by my childhood caregivers.

The realization slapped me in the face. I had been living without a mirror, and I realized that many confrontations resulted from not looking at myself first, not realizing that I was the problem. I learned that the opposite of ego is not low self-esteem, it is vulnerability. One closes the window to outside perspectives, and one opens it.

We went back to our hotel that evening and took a hot tub as we talked nonstop about us, our past, why past events happened and how each of us was committed to working on our issues in the future—our future.

Yet there were things unresolved. That night, spirits returned to me. It was the worst nightmare I'd had in a long time—maybe forever. I was sweating. It felt like evil spirits were attacking me. I woke up, and I went to the bathroom and locked myself in. I was hearing voices. They got louder and louder, and they were telling me that nothing ever changes. They were telling me all the things I had done wrong were going to remain inside of me. I would never be forgiven for all the smoking and drinking and lying.

The Psychic

On Day Three, we met with a psychic. My only other experience with a psychic was in Sedona three years earlier. Until that day, I didn't believe. We walked up to this little storefront in downtown Sedona, and there was a woman out front smoking. She followed us in and asked if we wanted a reading.

My wife said yes, and I went first. She told me to go into another room, sit down, and make myself comfortable. As I did that, I sat and turned around to face her as she followed me into the room. I swear she changed. I mean I just saw her fifteen seconds before in the lobby, and when I looked at her now, she was totally different. The room smelled sweet. Her persona and aura changed. It was really creepy.

"You don't believe, do you?" she asked.

I said no, I didn't believe in psychics. She looked me straight in the eyes and said, "I'm the real thing. This isn't BS. And I'm already hearing about you from the spirits. I'm already hearing what the spirits in this room are telling me about you."

Yeah, right. She was telling me how great she was, and then she interrupted herself, and she was looking around the room, up in the air, to the left and right. She appeared to be looking and listening to someone.

"Let me start with your past, then I will talk about today," she said. She paused and looked around again. I was getting a little weirded out at that point. That's when she started to tell me about my past, and there was no way she could have known those kinds of details.

She said she knew I had protected my mother from my father. She knew I almost died in college and that I can feel my mother's presence at certain times even though she had been dead for over twenty-five years. She knew about where I lived and about my brothers and sisters, about me being a loner as a child and even about my birth, how my family told me I was hatched rather than born. How did she know that? I was sitting there thinking, *What's going on?*

I tried joking about it, but then she reminded me, "I'm the real thing." It literally looked like she was listening to people talk to her in the room. "Your spirits are telling me that you're going to get your dream job that you have been working toward for a very long time." She started about how my wife, and I live in Colorado and that we had previously lived in Maryland. It literally looked like she was listening to people talk in the room. Then she asked me how she was doing. "Does this seem possible," she asked. I sat there in a daze.

That's what I was thinking about when we spoke to the psychic during our retreat. We were sitting outside on her beautiful deck. Immediately as she sat down, I mean before she actually got to her seat, she started looking up and around, left and right, as if she were looking and listening to people, we couldn't see. I was getting flashbacks from my other reading back in Sedona. She immediately told us there were spirits present that she was channeling.

They were telling her that our spirits have been traveling through time together, through many, many different lives over many, many years. Through it all, everything was planned and organized to finally get us to the present point in time.

She told us we'd been rich and poor. We've been different nationalities, lived in different time periods. She continued to tell us things about ourselves that she couldn't have known without some sort of prior knowledge. She continued to look up and around and was listening to voices, and she went on to tell me about my life and my past lives and about what my future entailed.

She said that I would use my skills of teaching and coaching to help young men who were having challenges in their lives, that I would be connected to several young men in the next several years that would need my help.

She said my future will be full of joy, as I would help young people deal with the world and their personal challenges. She said she understood my dependencies, my vices, my past, my future, all the things that I had done wrong—getting kicked out of college, having problems with family. She understood that I was a loner and about the times I was almost killed.

She also said the spirits wanted me to write a book that could be used to help others overcome what I have experienced, so they might know that they are not alone.

She told my wife about how she has a group of women that seemed to be gathered around her and do things like sports or games or anything like that. My wife described how she had a group of friends she skied and socialized with. The psychic said that because my wife was so good-natured and because of her spirit and desire to have fun and adventure, that she will use all of these things to help other women, whether it be one or two or even a group of women. She said my wife would help them and lead them to fun activities and happy days, which these women really need and look up to you for.

She ended by telling us that through all of our lives, this was to be the best time for our souls and our spirits, that it has taken us years and generations to get to where we were today.

Breathing

That afternoon, we had separate sessions called Breath and Sound. I took my wife to her appointment, then I drove to mine. I didn't know exactly what the exercise was about, and I was a bit nervous, but the woman running the session made me feel at home.

The breathing expert explained how to use my breath and air to relax my mind and body, which would allow me to take a journey into my inner soul. She taught me to breathe properly and do jaw exercises to relax the muscles around my mouth. She said the exercise would last a couple hours and that she was going to blindfold me so that I was in total darkness. Then she would place headphones on my ears. I didn't know what to think or expect.

She had me lay down on the bed, take deep breaths, and think about the rhythm of waves hitting the beach. She said that if I stopped breathing correctly, she would tap me on the chest to remind me to breathe deeply.

Through headphones I heard wild animals and African drums, spiritual prayers and sounds of native tribes dancing around fires. There were sounds of crying people, praying people, people chanting. I had never heard anything like it. I found myself using my arms to dance just like I do at Dead concerts. I was in full meditation. I saw bright lights inside my black mask, changing colors, a bright white light, circles getting bigger and smaller, and yellows and greens.

Even to this day, I don't remember everything that occurred during those two hours, but I do remember the last sounds I heard were from a song called, "Calling All Angels." I'd never heard the song, but I listened to the words, guitars and gospel singers. And I began to weep.

As I lay there weeping, the counselor said: "Lance, do not worry about moving right now. Do not remove your blindfold. Lie there until you're ready to wake up." She continued in a very quiet voice to tell me, "Just relax. Don't worry about moving. Let it out."

She told me it was natural and that I had just been reborn. It was exactly what I was feeling. It took me a good 20 to 30 minutes to finally get control over my emotions. I slowly took off the blindfold, and it was like waking up to a bright light after you've been sleeping for twenty hours. I couldn't see, and it took me a while to focus. It was truly a rebirth.

When I came out of that breathing exercise, I was a completely different person. Everything had changed. I felt that I had seen God, I saw something beyond. My whole state of mind completely changed at that point.

Every night before I go to sleep and, in the morning, when I wake up now, I pray in my own way, thanking God, thanking, whomever. I don't necessarily call him God, but I just say, "Hey, thank you." I'm much more spiritual than I ever was, and I still do the Hawaiian prayer: I'm sorry. Forgive me. Thank you. I love you.

I've learned a channeling process that has a couple of statements. Then it has a couple admissions and then I say, "I'm reaching on benefit of myself, and all involved. Is there anyone here to talk to me today?" Other times, I just kind of lie there, literally just look up and ask, "Who wants to talk?"

I told my wife when we met back up that I actually had a transcendental experience where I connected directly with the spirit world, and I literally transformed.

My wife had done the exercise before. What was unique about this time was that she felt vibrations in her body that she had never felt before. She actually had a point where she felt as if her blood was boiling, and then she was able to connect with her inner child, and she felt protected. It was an incredible meditation experience.

At the hot tub that night, we just relaxed and talked about our great day with the psychic reading and breathing exercises. As we sat in the hot tub, we chatted and giggled and talked about how the trip had made us more aware of internal issues that have impacted how we acted toward each other and how we could do better and better.

We went to bed, but woke again at 2 a.m. It had become our routine. It was during this conversation that we told each other how lucky we were and how much we loved each other and how we both understood that everything that had occurred during the last 25 years together happened in order to bring us to where we were that day.

It wasn't an accident the way we met, the way we moved from Baltimore to D.C. and to western Maryland, how we tried to have kids for four years using every medical procedure possible and then moving to Colorado where she had always dreamed of living, followed by the shock of losing my job and moving to Atlanta then back to Frisco.

And then, all the way through my snowboarding near death experience, through the construction project, it was all planned, planned to bring us to this day, to this town and this adventure, to this hotel. We felt that we were where we were supposed to be, and that we would do whatever we could to move forward together.

We talked for a few more minutes, and after telling each other how much we loved each other, we went back to sleep, holding each other tightly and waiting for the next day.

Final Day

It began with massages in the morning. Then we were scheduled to wrap things up in the afternoon. I hit the hot tub and did a few laps in the pool before we headed to our massages. The masseuses asked what kind of massage we wanted, and my wife said she preferred deep massages, so I asked for the same. They explained that we should feel free to breathe deeply, and if we felt pain to let them know. There were only a few times I had to yell as she hit some places in my legs, back and shoulders, which shot pain all through my body.

My wife was very quiet. Later, we talked about how the experience was just what we needed. We had spent the last three days cleansing, expanding, and relieving our souls and our minds and our pasts. We got our toxins rubbed out of our bodies, and we were feeling much better.

We went back to the hotel and, of course, got back into the hot tub before going back to the room to get dressed for our last session. We went to the same house we went to at the beginning of our four days. When we opened the door, we found both of our counselors standing their smiling, and they greeted us like long-lost family.

One of the counselors asked us how things had gone, if we had anything that we wanted to ask or talk about. We both said that we didn't have questions but that I did have a revelation of sorts. There were parts of my past that I hadn't remembered until that weekend. It was during the rock-crushing exercise, when I told the Shaman about how someone had shut me in a room and masturbated in front of me. I didn't even know what was going on. I kind of buried it and hadn't remembered it until that walk up the creek.

After a brief review of the week. The counselors conducted an exercise to activate our subconscious and find out what may or may not be hiding in our inner souls. They gave us little pads to hold between our thumbs and forefingers. The pads pulsated back and forth from hand to hand. As we held the pads, the counselors asked us questions.

I was asked when I felt powerless, and I said it was when I heard my father beating my mother, my mother trying to kill herself. The counselor asked if there were others, and I told her about how my mother told me that she and Dad would not get a divorce because they didn't want to do that to me, and of course about the guy who sexually assaulted me.

The counselor continued: "And when you felt powerless, what else did you think?"

"I was confused," I said. The conversation continued around the powerless feelings and in general how I felt responsible for the bad things I had experienced, and how I felt that I didn't matter. My life didn't matter to anyone. I wasn't important.

The counselor connected the dots, and I realized that everything I experienced as a child made me think that I didn't matter. It was just as clear to me as anything.

Twenty minutes into my wife's dive into her subconscious session, she kept asking them to rephrase questions to help her understand. I saw confusion on her face like I used to see during our arguments about the construction project. It made me sad. I thought to myself, "That was the face of what I called checking out." She was checking out and simple questions were confusing her. Then I noticed the two counselors looking at each other and passing notes.

Suddenly out of nowhere they stopped the exercise and asked her to drop the pulses, take off the blindfolds and open her eyes. They said they believed that they have just uncovered something very serious. And that they felt very strongly that my wife had something known as receptive expressive disorder, which they had only seen two or three times during the last 25-years-plus of marriage counseling. Two of those cases were in the past couple months.

They explained that it was a communication disorder that prevents people from hearing and understanding what is being said and causes difficulty in responding effectively. They asked her if she had issues in the past with understanding what people asked her. She said that it was true all her life. She said that in school, the teacher would talk, and she would hear the first sentence and all the rest was "womp, womp, womp, womp."

I thought about what had happened between us during the past couple years and probably all through our entire relationship. Up until a month earlier, I was so stoned and checking out all the time, I was oblivious.

As we sat there, I could see my wife beginning to cry. I reached over grabbed her hand and said, "Everything's going to be fine. We're going to work this out. Don't worry. It's probably nothing. Don't give it a second thought."

One of the causes of the disability is trauma to the head, and a couple days later, on our way back to Colorado, out of know where she remembered an incident in elementary school in which she and her classmates were playing a game during recess and one of them pushed her backwards, shattering a stained-glass window with her head. It all was beginning to make sense.

Our last session of the retreat was with our angel, who asked us what commitments we could make to each other. He asked us to use one word to describe our experiences. I said, "Inspirational," and my wife said, "Rebirth."

Then he had one final question. He asked us to complete this sentence: "Before this adventure…"

My wife said, "I was unheard. I was empty and without purpose. I was misguided and hid those things by keeping busy and having fun. Lance really does have my back. He understands me. Now I'm on a journey of discovery."

My response was, "I was detached, ego-driven, and self-protective. I was lost and afraid. I was on the wrong route. Now I'm focused and directed. I value myself and I feel compassion. I'm driven by goals and plans."

With that our weeklong adventure was over. That night we had a great meal, another hot tub and pool session, and then went to bed. It had been a whirlwind four days in which I learned a great deal about my wife, our relationship, and myself. We were closer than before. We could laugh more, enjoy each other more.

That night, there were more voices. I started to shout at them, and I fought with them until it woke up my wife. I went into the bathroom and locked the door behind me. The voices were getting louder and louder. I was going crazy. The voices kept repeating awful things. My wife came to the locked door and knocked and asked what was going on. "Are you OK? Are you OK?" she asked.

I told her to please leave me alone, that I was hearing voices and I was scared, and I didn't know what to do. I just kept screaming and crying, and then I went quiet. I started repeating the Hawaiian prayer: I'm sorry. Please forgive me. Thank you. I love you.

The spirits kept talking to me, and there was all this chatter in my head before I finally regained control. I could hear crying outside the door.

I opened the door and my wife was on the floor next to the door. She got up and gave me a big hug and held me. She put me in bed and spooned me and comforted me, telling me it was going to be OK.

The next morning, we talked about it, and I told her what the spirits were saying and how they wouldn't stop chattering in my ear. She listened to me and heard me and comforted me. The tools we learned already were helping us connect.

Later that morning, we were checking out of the hotel and anxious to get on the road. We planned on stops at Zion National Park and Bryce Canyon National Park in Utah on our way back to Colorado. We have always loved road trips. We don't even listen to music. We just talk, and it seems as though we appreciate each other more.

We talked about our adventure and how helpful and exciting it was. She was looking up spiritual sayings on her phone. It was beautiful. The scenery was spectacular. We talked and laughed and discussed everything, but there still were a couple things we hadn't talked about. We left Sedona, each of us knowing we still held secrets.

We arrived at Zion National Park through this really long tunnel. It was so long, I started feeling a little weirded out, but at the end of the tunnel, it was beautiful. Our conversation drifted to the incident in which she crashed through the window and how that might be the cause of her newly discovered disorder.

A few miles down the road, she brought up the topic of boundaries and how she was taught by her mother to delineate acceptable and non-acceptable behavior. It made me realize that I had never been taught about boundaries. How often had I acted and thought without regard to going too far, or allowing others to do the same to me?

I had lived with a sense of abandon. It was present when I played rugby or rode down a mountain on a snowboard. I considered boundaries to be restrictive, limiting my freedom and limiting my potential.

But now I was realizing that wasn't always the case. It was an important realization, because it helped us understand that we should stay within our own lanes and hope that others do the same.

It's when we drive across the center line, miss an exit or drive recklessly that we crash. There were times when my wife's interaction with other men made me feel uneasy and angry. We were always arguing about it.

She always said it was jealousy, but the discussion about boundaries confirmed that it wasn't. I was merely saying honestly what I had observed and how it made me feel. She said she understood why those instances might make me feel hurt. It was a huge breakthrough.

Through communication, respect and honesty, combined with the love we already felt for each other, we were determined to solidify one of the most important lessons we learned in Sedona: to be each other's wingmen.

I have an innate ability to know my way around an area even though I have never been there. I take pride in never missing a turn, but I didn't apply that to the rest of my life; and I have to admit that emotionally I have been lost for much of it, sometimes without even knowing it. I have felt great pain in my life, and much of it was because of someone breaking boundaries and failing to recognize how much of an effect it had on me.

We told each other we heard what the other person was saying and understood and agreed that boundaries would set a course for us to avoid causing each other pain and anger. It was a beautiful moment, but we both knew we were still withholding secrets.

We returned to the hotel, and, of course, went straight for the hot tub. We were getting along so well. In the hot tub, she brought up the night before. She had waited patiently until I was ready to talk about it. I told her voices were telling me that they still had me in their grip.

The next day, we headed to Bryce National Park and stopped for a short hike, several miles long. It was unbelievably beautiful. We hiked to a place called Inspiration Point, which seemed a perfect place. There were reddish colored spirals, rock formations that resembled sandcastles. They were hundreds of feet in height, and they were everywhere, as far as the eye could see.

Beautiful Bryce National Park

10

CONFESSIONS

We were headed to our hotel for the last night before returning to Colorado when my wife said she wanted to tell me something, but I had to promise not to get mad.

"What? What is it? What is it that she needs to tell me that I have to promise not to freak out? What's going on? Okay, this sounds serious. Let me pull over and stop driving."

I pulled over, and she asked if I remembered when she and her sister went skiing at Telluride a couple years earlier. I said yes. She asked if I remembered when we took a ski trip to Austria. I said yes again.

Then she asked if I remembered meeting a couple of American ski patrollers in Austria. I did. She explained how she ran into one of the patrollers from Austria in Telluride, and he asked her to join him for Happy Hour. She said her sister didn't want to go with her, so she joined him alone, and they had dinner.

She continued by saying that they were having a good time and that she made out with him.

I said, "What? How did it just jump from a happy hour at dinner to making out? What are you talking about?"

She said they went back to his place, and they were getting intimate before she started getting uncomfortable and left. She said how sorry she was and how much she regretted it. She explained that given her adventure this past week and how much I had admitted and all the things I let out, she felt she had to confess as well.

We got back in the car in the Middle of Nowhere, Utah. I was really not feeling well. She knew it. I was upset, and I continued to think about what I just heard and was trying to stay calm. After about twenty minutes, I had to stop driving. I spotted a safe place off the road and pulled over. I got out of the car and began to take a walk because I needed some air. I kept walking then stopped and stared at the mountains and desert in front of me. They seemed to go on forever.

She got out of the car after several minutes and slowly made her way to me. She saw the tears in my eyes and explained that nothing happened and that she realized what she had done and left him. She said that she didn't know why she had done it and wished it had never happened. I let her talk because I was just trying to stay calm and process her statements.

I had just learned over the last few weeks about compassion, about understanding, about not letting the ego take over. I finally started to talk and ask her questions. She answered everything. I could see her remorse and how she regretted what had happened and how she felt she had to tell me despite how I might take it. She was very sorry. And with that I said, "Done. We'll move ahead."

We stood in the middle of nowhere and held each other tightly for a very long hug. I had forgiven her. After some kissing, more hugs, we jumped back in the car.

Later we stopped at a hotel we reserved earlier. But when we got there and to our room. It was really, really a creepy hotel room. So, after dinner and a couple hours of sleep. We both woke up at the same time in the middle of the night. Looked at each other and said: "We are out of here!" And without saying another word we packed up the car and got out of that creepy room and drove through the night.

As we drove down the road, we talked about how successful our trip was, how we both felt we were back on track. We acknowledged we still had work to do, and we were ready to do it. We still needed to work on being better to ourselves and each other, but our marriage was saved, and we talked about how happy and grateful and lucky we were.

When we got over the Colorado line, we pulled over and stopped the car. It was daybreak so we got out to watch the sunrise, and just as the sun came over the horizon, we started dancing. We danced in circles as we laughed and hugged each other in joy. It was six in the morning. Truckers were going by and blowing their horns as we continued to laugh and tear up. It was a new day, a new beginning.

We picked up Kimba from a friend's house and arrived home around 4 p.m. Upon our arrival, we smudged our house with burning sage. There had been so much arguing during the project we wanted to get rid of those bad energies. We were going to do anything and everything we could to keep ourselves going in the right direction, from the burning of sage to the placement of crystals around the house and placing special rocks by the door to keep out evil spirits.

That night, we were still excited. As we lay in bed thinking about all that had happened, we just laughed at life and thought, "You can't make this shit up."

I didn't tell her that I was hearing more voices, that despite the laughter, I was going back into a zombie state. I didn't eat on Sunday. I did meditation and breathing exercises. But I wasn't able to fall asleep and I didn't move all that night.

It was early morning of Monday, June 5, when I woke up screaming as loudly as I could in the bedroom. I was fighting and arguing with the spirits. I started saying the Hawaiian prayer, and suddenly the voices stopped.

The nightmares were increasing in depth and frequency. That night, my wife woke me up and asked, "Are you OK? What's going on? What was your nightmare about?"

I told her there were spirits telling me there was one last confession, one last thing I had to tell her in order for us to move forward.

"What are you talking about?" she asked.

I told her I had a secret that I had to tell her, and that I wouldn't blame her if she got up and walked out on me and divorced me and left me forever. She had a look of fear on her face.

I had hidden it for years, many years, and I regretted it every day. "Last night the spirits told me that I had to let this out. I must tell you! I feel like dying, and I'm so sorry. I have one last confession." I told her I had cheated on her. She had a look of shock on her face that made me feel even worse. I saw the look on her face and knew it was over.

"What are you talking about? When did you do this?" She asked.

I told her that when I did it doesn't matter. What matters is that I must tell you that I cheated on you. For what it's worth. I never had any ongoing relationship, and I seriously regretted every doing it. And regardless of any influence alcohol or drugs had on me. There is no excuse for what I have done. I am very, very sorry.

She just sat there, then asked, "What now?"

"That's up to you, and I fully expect you to pack your bags and leave." Then I heard the spirits: *You've got to go climb a mountain. Get out of this house. Climb Peak 1!*

The Climb – Peak 1

I didn't fully understand what they were saying, but I knew they were referring to Peak 1 located on the 10 Mile Mountain Range. Breckenridge ski resort is located on Peak 6 through 10. It's a long hike, and it would give my wife time to be alone. I told her I was taking Kimba to climb the mountain, and she became very concerned. She said I was not in physical or mental condition to do such a dangerous hike. I explained that the spirit's voice told me to go and that I had no choice.

"Don't go. You'll hurt yourself." She made me promise not to do anything crazy. "And you know what I mean by crazy," she said.

The missing word was "suicide."

Was she right? I don't know. I thought by the end of our conversation, I could go up and slide off. I kind of thought about it. My mind wasn't stable. I thought this would be a great way. It could happen so easily. There are canyons where avalanches occur, and snow sticks up there in thin, little canyons, and I could just slide down.

I told her I had thought about it, really thought about it, and I told her that if she promised to be here when I returned, I would come back. I wouldn't do anything. She insisted I take Kimba, knowing that the two of us would keep each other safe.

We hiked up above the timberline. In areas there were four to five feet of snow on the ground. It was very steep, and a careless mistake could result in a 2,000-foot fall. I reached the top in about four hours, and the spirits were waiting for me.

We had a conversation like none I had ever had. I sat there talking on top of the mountain, making promises, making commitments and telling them, "Thank you." I told them I was sorry that I tried to hide the secret. I fought myself, I gave my prayers. I did everything I could to forgive myself.

How often has it been said that on the top of a mountain, one is closer to God? That day, almost 14,000 feet above sea level, I completed my transformation. I left Peak 1 with the same amount of pain, but my burden seemed less. All told, it was almost eight hours before I reached the bottom. It was an incredible journey, a long, tough climb to find forgiveness, hope, and... myself.

When I arrived home, she was still there. She accepted me and my apologies and said, "I'm not fully over this and I may never fully get over this! But with everything else I've done and you've done, I will forgive you. I do forgive you! And I will do my best to try and forget everything, and we will move forward."

In my life, faith has restored what I could not. Smoking marijuana was a decision I made without considering its effects on me and those around me. Maybe I was weak or selfish. Faith has given me strength and an understanding that nothing happens by coincidence. We face barriers to learn that we can overcome them. The result is a life more abundant than we thought possible.

There still are moments, however, when loving myself doesn't seem possible and I feel like giving up. I tell myself that maybe I will get it right the next time. I still turn to the mountain and the prayer hoping to overcome demons.

I am a part-time professional snowboarding instructor now, and it allows me to connect with people. It's a wonderful feeling to see students go from learning to strap on their boards to reaching the top of the mountain for the first time so that they might look around them, absorb inspiration and truly understand what getting high is all about.

I feel now that I finally have become a man, a good man. And better yet, a good husband. It wasn't through football or rugby; it was through vulnerability and the unwillingness to allow ego to hide truth. I can say now that if truth matters, I matter.

Perhaps that's what the spirits have been saying all along.

Kimba and me on Peak 1

About The Author

The author of this book never thought he would ever be a published writer. And to this day he still can't believe he is. From the very beginning of his life, he had to fight to survive. He was born eight weeks early in an age when preemie babies didn't make it. But he did. And that fight for life has never left his soul.

LB (the author) grew up in a modest home playing outdoors, working hard in school, and listening to his parents. His childhood memories seemed normal and ordinary until later in his life when he began to have nightmares and he started hearing voices. Voices that he remembered hearing as a child.

As a child he didn't really think much of the voices and thought that everyone heard them. Then in his teenage years he started to smoke pot and the voices drifted away. And by this time, he didn't even notice them leaving.

LB went on to college and played sports. In was during college where he almost died for the second time in his life. This time it was from a knee injury he got playing football that became seriously infected with gangrene. He survived this near-death experience with the help of a dying girl who held his hand and gave him her soul. LB will never forget this young woman and to this day thinks of her and preys to her often.

After college LB worked various jobs before beginning his career. It was around this time that he met the women of his dreams who would later become his wife. She was a beautiful soul with a lot of spirit, who loved to have fun, and who was outgoing and athletic. Of course, all along LB still smoked pot every day. Pot was LB's remote control. It was with him every day like his best friend, his go to for help, and the crutch that he didn't even know he used.

Later in his life LB and his wife moved far away from their families on the East coast to the mountains of Colorado. Where they lived in vacation land, enjoyed the outdoors and their beautiful world. It was here that LB almost died for a third time snowboarding off a cliff and landing at the bottom of a tree. The fall off the cliff shattered his leg and ankle into multiple pieces. But he was alive.

As he laid at the bottom of the tree that broke his fall. He realized how fast life can be taken away without even a blink of the eye. He sat there and connected with God as tears ran down his face. It was shortly after this third near-death experience that he starts hearing the voices again. And the voices he was hearing were not good. The more he smoked pot the worse the voices sounded. It was also at this time that he and his wife became having major marital issues which stemmed from poor communications. She couldn't hear what he was saying as he kept smoking pot to live in his own world.

LB and his wife desperately needed help. He is now hearing evil voices that are attacking him and he is experiencing seriously violent nightmares. His wife starts searching for help for their relationship and for LB's issues. She locates a group in Sedona that she thinks can help save their relationship and at the same time possibly LB's life. It was during this time that LB was out walking their dog one afternoon when he heard a different voice. And this voice he recognized. It was the calming safe sound of the voice he had heard as a young child and teenager. The trusting voice his grandfather once told him to never leave and to always listen. And who he hadn't heard since he started smoking pot some 42 years earlier.

As he walked his dog the voice became more and more clear. LB drifted into a mild trance and was now being led around the neighborhood by his dog.

The voice he heard told him that he had to stop smoking pot, immediately. And that if he stopped smoking pot, he would get his life and his wife back. The voice he was hearing was the same one that he had not heard for many, many years. The voice was making him a deal. A deal he couldn't refuse.

About the Book

The Project – "a story of addictions overcome by faith" is about a person who overcame a terribly challenging childhood that made him not love himself and respect his life. A childhood that he buried in his past with the help of a daily addiction to marijuana. His challenges never let up through his teenage and young adult years. His loss of self to his addictions caused major issues throughout college, his career, and his marriage. He left his connection to faith and his beliefs in God as a young teenager and it took 42 years for him to find his way back. The return of faith back to his life was not an easy journey. After several near-death experiences, major marital issues that nearly led to a divorce, and several battles with the evil spirt world. The main character of this story finds himself just in time before his destruction. The driver to the change in his life is a reborn connection to God. God reached out and talked to him and he was ready to listen and make the necessary changes. Changes that included ending an addiction to marijuana after 42 years of daily use.

Through the challenging experiences that he overcame with the help of faith and God. The main character learns to love himself, that truth always comes out, and to believe that God is always in control.